Vanya

Simon Stephens

methuen | drama

LONDON • NEW YORK • OXFORD • NEW DELHI • SYDNEY

METHUEN DRAMA
Bloomsbury Publishing Plc
50 Bedford Square, London, WC1B 3DP, UK
1385 Broadway, New York, NY 10018, USA
29 Earlsfort Terrace, Dublin 2, Ireland

BLOOMSBURY, METHUEN DRAMA and the Methuen
Drama logo are trademarks of Bloomsbury Publishing Plc

First published in Great Britain 2023

Cover design & photography: feastcreative.com

A catalogue record for this book is available from the British Library.

A catalog record for this book is available from the Library of Congress.

ISBN: PB: 978-1-3504-4341-9
ePDF: 978-1-3504-4343-3
eBook: 978-1-3504-4342-6

Series: Modern Plays

Typeset by Mark Heslington Ltd, Scarborough, North Yorkshire

To find out more about our authors and books visit
www.bloomsbury.com and sign up for our newsletters.

VANYA
After Chekhov

Adapted by Simon Stephens

Co-created by Simon Stephens, Andrew Scott, Sam Yates, and Rosanna Vize

Performed by Andrew Scott

Vanya opened at Richmond Theatre on 28 August 2023, before transferring to The Duke of York's Theatre, London, on 21 September, and was produced by Wessex Grove, Gavin Kalin Productions, and Kater Gordon. The creative and production teams were as follows:

Creative Team

Director: Sam Yates
Designer: Rosanna Vize
Lighting Designer: James Farncombe
Sound Designer: Dan Balfour
Video Designer: Jack Phelan
Movement Director: Michela Meazza
Music: Kelly Moran
Costume Designer: Natalie Pryce
Associate Designer: Blythe Brett
Assistant Director: Francesca Hsieh
Props Supervisor: Kate Margretts
Understudy: Victoria Blunt

Production Team

Production Manager: Juli Fraire
Company Stage Manager: Martin Hope
Deputy Stage Manager: Imogen Firth
Assistant Stage Manager: Timesha Mathurin
Sound No. 1: Erik Jackson
Sound No. 2: Alice Brooks
Wardrobe Manager: Jordan Colls
Lighting Operator: Jeannie Fong
Technical Swing: Kj Barham
Marketing Director & Associate Producer: Bonnie Royal for Roast Productions
Press & Publicity: Kate Morley PR
Rehearsal & Production Photographer: Marc Brenner
Artwork: Feast Creative
Producer & General Manager: Wessex Grove

Vanya

Simon Stephens

**A version of *Uncle Vanya* by
Anton Chekhov**

Characters

Michael
Maureen
Ivan
Alexander
Helena
Liam
Sonia
Elizabeth

All the roles are performed by one actor.

Act One

An early afternoon in June.

A veranda by a garden.

Michael *and* **Maureen**.

Maureen   Have a cup of tea, Michael.

Michael   I don't really feel like tea, Maureen.

Maureen   Maybe you should have a 'drink' drink, Michael.

Michael   No.

I don't drink every day you know, Maureen. I don't drink, like, all the time.

This weather. It feels like it's going to break.

How long have we known each other 'Reeny?

Maureen   God. Let me think. You came here for the first time, when was it, when Anna, Sonia's mother was sick? Then you had to come again the following year. Two visits in two years before she died.

So that's eleven years ago.

Michael   Have I changed do you think?

Maureen   Oh yeah. You really have. You used to be handsome. You were so young then. Now you're old.

And, you know, you're not as pretty as you used to be. And you drink more than you used to.

Michael   Yeah.

In this last ten years I have turned into an entirely different person. And do you know why that is, Maureen? It's because I've worked myself to the bone, that's why. I'm on my feet all day. I never rest. And then. You know. You go to bed at night. You pray to God that nobody's going to call you in the middle of the night. But they do. In all the time I've known you. This whole last decade. I've not had one day off. What do you expect me to do but get old? And then life – Isn't it? It's stupid. It's shitty. It drags you down. And you look around you and all you can see are lunatics. The people here are lunatics. Every one of them. If you're surrounded by lunatics, well, after a while, Maureen, after a while you turn into a lunatic yourself.

I've grown a moustache. How has that happened? A really stupid moustache. See, 'Reeny. I've turned into a lunatic too. It's not that I'm stupid. I'm not stupid yet thank you very much. My brain's still largely in the right place. But my, my, my feelings. My feelings are dull and dead. I don't want anything. I don't need anything. I don't love anybody.

Except for you, 'Reeny. I love you.

Maureen   Are you sure you don't want a drink?

Michael   Yes. I am, thank you, 'Reeny.

At the end of March, I went to, there was a family I went to visit. There were rumours they'd been infected with – I don't know. These rumours. These people. The way they lived. They slept squashed up. They were lying so close together. Side by side. The filth. The stench. The smoke. There were animals, I don't know, dogs and rats and all manner of – crawling around the people on the floor. I worked that whole day. I didn't stop. Didn't sit down. Didn't eat. I got home and there was a call from a woman who was a neighbour of mine. Her husband, a young guy, was – he was very sick. She wanted to know if I would see him. She didn't want him to go into the hospital. I should have insisted but – she asked me if they could come round. So I let them. He was in a great deal of pain. He was very sick. His lungs and his liver and his bones. I needed to anaesthetise him to examine him. I was very tired. He died, 'Reeny, while I was examining him. Suddenly. I didn't expect it to, 'Reeny, but – you know? It got to me. It did.

I felt like I'd killed him on purpose.

I sat down. I hid my face. Here. Like this.

And I find myself thinking. The people who come after us in a hundred years' time. In two hundred years' time. Those people who – We're making a world for them. What will they say about us? Will they have anything good to say about the things we did? They won't, 'Reeny. You know that don't you?

Maureen Well, Michael, they may not remember us at all. But God will.

Michael I see. Yes. Thank you, 'Reeny. I don't quite know what to say about that.

Ivan *enters.*

Ivan Right.

Right.

Michael, you're back.

Michael Ivan, good afternoon! You get some sleep?

Ivan Yes.

Yes, I did. I slept very well.

He yawns.

Ever since Alexander the Great got here. And his good wife. They've completely knocked our life out of kilter. I sleep really deeply at absolutely the wrong times of day. I eat all this weird food. From, like, Kabul. I'm serious. I drink wine in the day. It's not good for me, really. Before, they got here I never had a spare moment. Me and Sonia were working all the time. Managing the orders. Preparing the boxes. Managing the deliveries. We really were! But now it's just Sonia who's working because all I do is sleep, eat, drink, repeat, sleep, eat, drink, sleep, repeat, eat . . . It's not good for me at all.

Maureen It's ridiculous, Ivan. Alexander gives me these instructions about the food that he can eat when he's working. He wants me to make him soup. He insists that I make him fresh soup every day which makes no sense because soup is not exactly very difficult to keep but, no, he wants it fresh. So, I do. I make him soup. He gets up at midday and works right through the afternoon. And the soup gets cold, and he complains about it being reheated. Before he got here, we had lunch every day at one o'clock. Like normal people do. Now we're waiting for him to give the word. With those two, lunch is after six some days! At night all he ever does is read and write and then. One o'clock in the morning. He calls me. Good Lord. 'What on earth do you want?' 'Mineral water! I need iced mineral water!' I'm dragged out of bed just to find him some iced mineral water. It's. Honestly! I have no words!

Michael   Ivan, How long do you think they'll be here?

Ivan   About a hundred years.

It's like now! The soup was ready when he asked for it. And they've just gone for a 'walk'! A walk! 'My name's the Maestro and I'm going for a walk!'

This is them! Shush. They're coming.

Alexander, **Helena** *and* **Liam** *enter.*

Ivan   Alexander! Helena! Welcome home from your perambulations!

Alexander! Have some soup!

Alexander   Not if it's been sitting.

Ivan, my dear chap, would you be so kind as to bring me some hot tea to my study. There's a scene I need to finish by the end of today. Helena, help me upstairs. My leg is absolute murder.

Helena *and* **Alexander** *go into the house.*

Ivan   It's boiling hot. And it's stuffy. Stuffy is the precise word for what it is. But he puts his coat on and his thermals and his mittens.

But Helena? She's amazing. I think she might be the most beautiful woman I've ever seen in my life.

Liam   Do you know? Wherever I am in the countryside, guys . . .

Ivan   Liam! Where are you?

Liam   I'm here. I've been here all this time.

Wherever I am in the countryside, guys, whether that's striding, like, across the, the, the fields, Maureen, or walking through a garden or even sitting here. Out here. Now. On this little chair. With you. I feel such bliss. This weather is so lovely. The little, what are they? The little birds are singing. The way we live here. Simply. Happily. Peacefully. What else would anybody need out of life?

Michael   So what's been going on, Ivan?

Ivan   Nothing, Michael. Everything is exactly the same as it has always been. I'm the same as I've always been. Maybe a bit worse. My mother is still a mad old crow. Wittering on and on about feminist literary theory. She's got one eye on the grave and the other eye reading all these books about how at her age her life is just beginning.

Alexander sits all day in his study and writes and writes and writes. Scratching and scraping and crossing out and writing more. In a frenzy. It's the paper I feel sorry for. He's not made a single film for seventeen years, Michael. He's as dry as a bone. Withered by age. He is perennially suffering. His spleen is a tumour of envy and jealousy. And this old fucker is living on his first wife, my sister's money. Anna, may she rest in peace. And he's staying in her house on her potato farm not because he wants to but because he can't afford to live in the city. All he does is write increasingly indecipherable scripts that nobody will ever read and whine about how unlucky his life has been. The poor bastard.

When really. Really. The luck that man has had.

Seriously, Michael.

He's, what, the son of a farmer? And he's ended up, what do they call him? A generation-defining filmmaker. He's been given three honorary doctorates. Three?! Dr, Dr, Dr! And what for? For nothing. Nothing at all. Think about it. He's been going on and on and on for as long as I can remember about beauty in film and aesthetics in art. But he knows nothing about art. He understands nothing about art. Not a thing. He's never had an original idea in his life. Not a real, proper idea of his own. His only successful films were adaptations. And even they were, you know? Adequate. They weren't what I would call 'generation defining' for fuck's sake! And he's pompous. And he never fucking shuts up. And now he's publicly announced he's going into retirement? But nobody noticed because nobody gives a shit about him anymore. He's invisible. He's irrelevant.

And the luck that fucker has with women. Not even Don Juan de Marco had the luck he has.

Michael   'Don Juan'?

You met Anna.

Michael   I did.

Ivan   How beautiful was she?

Michael   She was very beautiful.

Really, though, Michael. She was. She was. She was lovely. A gentle thing. And she had so much love. The number of men who fell in love with my sister? But she loved *him*. Out of all of them. My mother worships him.

Her voice goes all weird when she talks to him. She looks at him like he's some kind of prophet. And now Helena. He's about a hundred and twenty-eight times older than she is. And look at her, Michael. The things she's throwing away just to be with him. Her youth. Her beauty. Her, her, her lustre. What for, Michael? Why would she do that?

Michael   Is she faithful to Alexander?

Ivan   Oh, she is. Even though he's so old and frail and decrepit and broken that every time he looks at her, she brings up a little bit of sick. The idea of a woman betraying a man like that? That would be awful. Clearly. But for a woman to sacrifice her whole life. That's perfectly acceptable. Clearly.

Liam   Ivan. Really. I don't like it when you get like this. Seriously. You know? You can't go round saying that anybody who betrays their, their, their husband or their wife isn't awful. It is. They are. You betray your husband. You betray your country. That's what I say.

I'm sorry, Ivan. My wife betrayed me, you know? Ran off with this man. Just because she loved him. Is what she said. The day after we got married! She said looking at him made her realise how ugly my skin was. She married him. But. And this is the important bit. Ever since. I have stayed true to her. I still love her, see? And I am completely faithful to her. I am. I give her whatever money I can. To help her raise her children, you understand. She had children with this man. She loved him. I told you that.

Ivan   You do what?

Liam   I might not have my happiness, Ivan. But I have my pride.

And the thing about her is? Her youth has gone. Her beauty has gone. As it does! The man she left me for, well, he's gone too, actually. She's got absolutely nothing.

Sonia *and* **Helena** *enter.* **Elizabeth** *follows.* **Maureen** *leaves.*

Michael   Helena! I'm confused.

You told me that your husband was very sick. You said he had rheumatism. He seems a picture of health to me.

Helena   He wasn't last night, Michael.

He was depressed. He had pains all down his legs, he said. But today he does seem a lot better.

Michael   I raced to get the train.

I came miles. Hundreds and hundreds of miles.

Helena   You didn't.

Michael   Oh well. Not the first time this has happened to me. Won't be the last. I can stay here.

At least I'll get a good night's sleep.

Helena   I hope so.

Michael   Is that alright, Sonia? Can I stay here? Sonia?

Sonia   Oh, of course you can, Michael. You never stay with us anymore. Have you eaten anything?

Stay and eat with us. We have lunch at six o'clock. That seems to be what we do nowadays.

This tea's cold.

Liam   It's the pot, Sonia. That particular pot gets hot very quickly. I noticed it. The pot gets hot. The tea gets cold.

Helena   Never mind, Ian, we'll have cold tea.

Liam   I'm so sorry, Miss Helena, I do beg your pardon. It's not Ian. It's Liam.

Or Crater. Some people call me Crater. On account of the marks on my face. I had acne when I was twelve. And not just spots. Really quite horrible acne. I think there are photos somewhere. It left these marks. And they look a bit like craters. On the, the, the moon.

Alexander, your husband, he knows me very well.

I live here now. You probably know that. It's your estate. Of course, you know that. You've probably noticed me, you know. Eating with you. Every day.

Sonia   Liam is our life saver, Helena. Our right-hand man. Our second in command.

Elizabeth   Oh! I forgot to tell Alexander. I'm losing my memory. Andrew Biederman sent me the new manuscript of his book.

Ivan   Super. Is it fascinating?

Elizabeth   Well. It's strange, Ivan. He's arguing against his own ideas. He writes about ideas he had seven years ago and how wrong headed and dated they were. And the things he says about Alexander's work. About all of our work. It's terrible really.

Ivan   That's not terrible at all. Changing your mind is a sign of thought, Mother. Nothing wrong with a spot of thought every now and then. Drink your tea.

Elizabeth   I'm talking, Ivan.

Does it irritate you to listen to me talk? To hear me think? You've changed, Ivan. I'm sorry but it's true. You have. I barely recognise you nowadays. You've become cynical. You had a good soul. You used to be so clear in your convictions. They used to shine from you.

Ivan   I know they did, Mother! My convictions used to positively radiate! I remember that so well!

They used to shine all over the fucking place.

'You had a good soul.'

Seriously, fucking no need for that.

Elizabeth   What's odd, Ivan, is that it's like you blame your misery on your convictions. Your convictions aren't the problem. You are. You never put your convictions into practice. You should have gone out and done something. You never did.

Ivan   Done something? Do you know how difficult it is to go out and just 'do something' nowadays? We can't all be generation-defining artists like your beloved fucking Alexander, Mother. We can't all have you at our beck and call. Bringing us drinks. Making us fucking salads.

Elizabeth   What are you implying, Ivan?

Sonia   Grandma. Uncle Ivan. Please.

Ivan   Sorry. I'm sorry, Sonia. I'll shut up. Not a word more from me.

Pause.

Helena   I love this weather.

It's not too hot is the thing I like about it.

Pause.

Ivan   It's the perfect weather to hang yourself in, I think. To be hung. Not to be hung. To be hanged.

Michael   If you ever have the chance you should come round to where I live. Come with Sonia. I'd love that.

My place is just small compared to here. But just by it there's a reserve. A public forestry reserve that I tend to.

Helena   I've heard about that. I don't know how you have time. You're a doctor, Michael. Your work's so important.

Michael   Oh who knows what's important in life, Helena?

Sonia   Michael's forest is amazing, Helena. He plants new trees every year. And the work he does to preserve the oldest trees there. You ask anybody. It matters. The forests matter. He told me once that trees teach humans what it is to be beautiful. In countries where there are more trees people don't fight against nature. They are more sensitive. Their language is softer. They treat women, they treat everybody more gently.

Michael   Our whole world is burning up. It will be gone forever. And we all know all this. We've known it for years. We just never do anything about it.

Only human beings have the capacity to create and to imagine things that don't exist but all we've ever done is destroy things. Maybe I'm losing my mind. When I plant, say, a birch tree and watch how it turns green or sways in the wind my soul fills with a kind of pride and I –

Helena   Aren't you a bit young? To be so bothered about by a load of old trees.

Michael   Ah fuck it. It's too late. We had our chance. We wasted it.

Sonia, I'm going to go.

Sonia   What? Already?

Michael   I can still get the last train if I go now.

Sonia   When will you come back, Michael?

Michael   I don't know, Sonia. That depends. Ask your father.

Sonia   Let me see you out at least.

They go into the house.

Helena   His face. The doctor. He looks so tired. He looks sensitive is how he looks. His face is. It's an interesting face. Sonia's obsessed. You can tell. She's so in love with him. In the time I've been here he's visited twice but the thing about me is that I'm shy. I haven't managed to speak openly with him until just now. He must have thought I was so rude. Don't look at me like that. I don't like it.

Ivan   How else am I meant to look at you?

Helena　I wish I had the slightest idea what it is that you want from me, Ivan.

What?

He struggles to stop himself from giggling.

Ivan　I just want to look at you. And you don't send me away. That's all I want. That all I need.

Helena　This, this is torture to me.

Act Two

July.

A dining room.

Two in the morning.

Alexander *and* **Helena**.

Alexander   Who's that? Sonia?

Helena   It's me, Alexander. Helena. Your wife.

Alexander   No don't close the window. I can barely breathe. I feel like I'm suffocating in here. I fell asleep. I dreamed that my leg didn't belong to me anymore. My left leg. What time is it?

I think I need to watch some Chaplin.

Helena, in the morning I want you to go and look in my collection for some films made by Charlie Chaplin. Do you know who he is? He's a filmmaker.

Why can't I breathe properly?

Helena   Because you're tired. You should be in bed.

Alexander   I hate getting old. Its repulsive. I'm so old now I've started to disgust myself.

And my God, you lot find it impossible even to look at me. I can see it in your faces.

I can see it in your face more than anybody else's you know? How repellent I am to you.

It must be absurd to you that I'm still alive. I know you hate fucking me.

Helena   That's not true, actually.

Alexander   I want my life back. The, the success. And the fame. And the love. And the attention. I want them back. I'm scared that I am going to die. I'm not strong enough to die, Helena.

Helena   It's okay. It's alright.

Sonia *enters.*

Sonia   Daddy, you ordered us to send for Michael. It was your idea. You insisted. So, we did. And he came. And now you refuse to see him.

Alexander   Sonia, what the hell would I want to see Michael for? He knows about as much about medicine as I know about fucking knitting.

Sonia   Fine. Suit yourself.

It makes absolutely no difference to me.

Some time.

Alexander   I'm bloody boiling. I'm absolutely boiling hot.

Sonia, pass me my tablets. From the table.

Not these ones. Did I ask you for these ones? No, I didn't.

Sonia   Are you having one of your tantrums, Dad? Well, it's very sweet, but there's no point having one with me. Some people might enjoy it, but I don't have the time. I've got to get up early tomorrow. Come on. He should be in bed.

Alexander   I'm not having a tantrum. I'm the only truly happy one in the whole bloody house.

Sonia   Come on. Let's go.

Alexander   Jesus!

Sonia   My legs ache too, Daddy.

I'll sort him, Helena. Don't you worry about it.

Sonia *leads* **Alexander** *out.*

Ivan *enters.*

Helena Jesus, Ivan.

Ivan The rain'll stop soon. And all the fields and everything in nature will start breathing again. I won't. I'll be the only thing for miles around not refreshed by the storm.

Helena Ivan, whenever you talk about things like your life and the things that you think I drift off completely. I don't know what to say to you. I'm sorry.

Goodnight, Ivan.

She stands to leave. He blocks her way.

Ivan, stop.

He blocks her with his arm.

Helena Will you get off my arm please? And for God's sake just leave me alone. It's horrible. It is.

She leaves.

Ivan She's gone.

I used to see her around, back in the day. Why didn't I do something then? Before he got to her. She'd be my wife!

Yes.

I have been tricked is the thing. I used to worship that man. The maestro. The things that I did for him. I worked like a horse. I did. I worked with Sonia. On the estate. We saved every penny, and sent it all to him, to keep him going. It's because I, and I don't tell this to many people, I was so proud of him. And his creative life. And the things that he created. I lived for them. Everything he made seemed like it was blessed. Like it was graced by a kind of genius. Jesus Christ. It's true. And now. He's here. And what has his life amounted to? What does it sum up to in the end? Nothing at all. A bubble of soap! He tricked me all along. I can see it now. I have been so stupid.

Michael *and* **Liam** *enter.*

Michael   Play us a song, Liam.

Liam   Everybody's asleep, Michael.

Michael   Come on, you fucking prick! Give us a tune!

Did I hear Helena?

She is. Just. Gorgeous.

Jesus. Look at all these pills. All these drugs. They're from all over the place. He's travelled the whole world boring the shit out of people with his fucking gout. Do you think he really is ill or is he just pretending?

What is the matter with you today, Ivan? Are you worried about Alexander's health now?

Or is it that you just want to fuck his wife?

Ivan   Your mind. It's filthy, Michael.

Michael   What? Well. Yeah. I must admit I am getting a bit filthy. The older I get. And. You might be able to spot this. I'm drunk too. When I get this drunk. I am just horrible. When I get like this, I don't care about anything, I'll take on any job. Don't care. I love you so fucking much.

Crater, I told you to play us a tune.

I could kill a drink. Come on, Ivan. I bet there's some brandy in here. Give it a few hours. Wait till the dawn breaks Then we can go – the boss at the Railway Arms. He said he'd serve me any time. Alright? I worked with a medical student once. He used to say, 'All wight?' He'd pronounce it like that. 'All wight?' He was such a prick. 'All wight?'

Sonia *comes in.*

Michael   Sonia. Sorry. I'm just going to . . .

Sonia   Hello.

Uncle Ivan, the potatoes have been harvested and all the orders are ready but we don't have the space to store them properly. This rain could ruin everything. They'll rot. Everything will rot. And you haven't even noticed. You've just completely stopped working. I'm working on my own. Uncle Ivan, are you crying?

Ivan   The way you looked at me. You reminded me so much of Anna. My beautiful sister. Where's she gone? If only she knew. If she knew.

Sonia   If she knew what?

Ivan   Everything is. It's very hard. It's not good. None of this. Never mind. Later. It's nothing. I'm going.

He goes.

Sonia   Michael? Are you out there? Can you come here please, Michael?

I don't mind how much you drink. As long as you don't make yourself sick. But don't let Uncle Ivan drink. It's not good for him.

Michael   Right. Yes. We won't drink any more. I'll go back home. I'll go now.

Sonia   Wait until the rain's stopped at least.

Michael   I'm going. I am.

And please. Sonia. Don't ask me to come and see your fucking father again. Today he wouldn't even look at me.

Sonia   It's because he's spoilt.

He's a big fat stupid baby.

Do you want something to eat, Michael?

Michael   Er. Okay. Yes. That would be good.

Sonia   We can have a midnight snack. I love a midnight snack, me. I think there's something in here.

Here. Have some cheese.

Michael   I've not actually eaten anything all day. I've only
drank. Drunk. Drank.

Sonia?

Sonia   Yeah?

Michael   There's no one else here. Can I be honest with
you?

Sonia   Okay . . .

Michael   Helena . . .

Sonia   What about Helena?

Michael   I'm not saying she's not beautiful. She is. She is
the fairest of them all. But all she does is eat, sleep, go for
little walks and swan about. Nothing more. She has no
responsibilities. She's idle. Idle people can never be truly
beautiful.

Sonia   Are you unhappy with your life, Michael?

Michael   No. I mean yes. I mean no. I love life. I love being
alive. In terms of my, my, my personal life? I mean Jesus.
There is absolutely nothing in it that is in the slightest bit
good. You know that feeling, when you walk through the
woods at night and you see a light, like a small light shining
in the distance and so then you don't notice your tiredness
anymore. Or the darkness. Or the sharp branches when they
hit you in the face. I'm sorry. It. Sometimes I do get. I get
quite depressed. And the thing is. There's no light in the
trees for me. It's been a long, long time since I cared for
anybody.

Sonia   Nobody?

Michael   I quite like Maureen.

Sonia   No, Michael, don't. Don't drink any more.

Michael   Why not?

Sonia   It doesn't suit you. You're so elegant. You have the gentlest voice. And, yeah, you're not like other people. I don't know anybody like you. I think you're wonderful. Stop it. Stop it. Please stop it, Michael.

Michael   Okay. I won't drink any more.

Sonia   Promise?

Michael   Promise.

Sonia   Thank you.

Michael   There. I'm done. I'm sober. Look. I've sobered up. I will stay like this until the day I die.

Sonia   Can I ask you something? If I had a friend. Or a, a, a younger sister, and you found out that. Well, say you found out that she was in love with you. What would you do?

Michael   I have no idea. I don't think I'd do anything.

Anyway.

If I'm going, I should go now. I'll say goodbye now, my love. Or we'll end up going on all morning.

He kisses her cheek.

I'm going to go out of this door if I can. I'm worried your uncle is lurking for me outside.

He goes out.

Sonia   Goodnight. That way.

He didn't say anything. It's so odd. He didn't say a word to me or tell me anything about any feelings he had for – or his – So why am I so happy all of a sudden?

I said to him, 'I think you're wonderful. You've got such a lovely voice.' Was that a bit inappropriate? His voice. It sings. I can feel it. In the air in this room. And then I said that thing about a younger sister and he didn't really get it. Oh. I hate that I am so ordinary looking. I'm so dull looking. It's true though. Last Sunday I was out in the village and I heard these two women and they were talking about me and I heard one of them say, 'she's such a good person and she's so kind but it's a shame because she just looks so ordinary.' Ordinary.

Helena   Sonia.

Sonia   Helena.

Helena   The rain's stopped. That air. It's amazing.

Sonia.

Sonia   Yes, Helena?

Helena   How long are you going to be in a huff with me? I don't understand it. I'm tired of it, Sonia. Isn't it about time we made friends?

Sonia   Yeah.

Let's not be cross with each other anymore.

Helena   Yes! Let's not!

Sonia   Has Daddy gone to bed?

Helena   No. He's sitting up in his room.

Who's been in here?

Sonia   Michael, he was having some cheese and crackers.

Helena   You're angry with me because you worried that I married your father for his money or his fame or something. If I swore to you, would you believe me? I swear I married him because I love him. I was attracted to him because he was so brilliant.

Sonia   If I asked you a question, Helena, would you answer me honestly? Are you happy?

Helena   No.

Sonia   I knew you weren't. Can I ask you another question? Tell the truth again. Do you sometimes wish your husband was younger?

Helena   Of course I do!

Ask another.

Sonia   Do you like the doctor?

Helena   Yes. Very much. Do you?

Sonia   Have I gone red, Helena? I have, haven't I?

He's so clever. He's amazing. I think he can do anything. He saves lives. He plants forests.

Helena   It's not about the forests, Sonia. And it's not about being a doctor either. My love, it's his soul. When he plants a tree he knows, he can see in his mind what it will be like in a thousand years. Most people aren't like that you know. Sometimes he can be a bit vulgar. And he drinks sometimes. But what does that matter? Can you blame him?

With all my heart, Sonia, I hope it works out for you. You deserve to be happy.

The thing about me is I'm so boring. I'm just an extra in other people's lives. With my music. In your father's world. In this place. I'm just a bit part character.

Why are you laughing?

Sonia   It's because I'm happy.

Helena   I'm going to play something. Right now.

Sonia   Oh. On my mother's piano?

Helena   Your father's still awake. You go and ask him. If he doesn't mind, then I'll play something for you.

Sonia   Yes, miss!

She goes out.

Helena   I've not played in such a long time.

The sound of the countryside from outside.

God I hate the countryside.

Sonia *enters.*

Sonia   He said you can't. You're not allowed to touch it.

Act Three

September.

Lunchtime.

The library.

Sonia, **Ivan** *and* **Helena**.

Helena I'm so bored. It's killing me. I don't know what I am meant to do with myself anymore.

Sonia I'm sure I could find you something.

Helena Like what?

Sonia There's work on the farm that you could do.

Helena Do I really look like the kind of woman who has the slightest idea how to work with potatoes?

Sonia You could get a job teaching in the village. Or you could volunteer to look after the sick. That's something you could do isn't it?

Helena Sonia, it's only in films that people go out and teach illiterate children or tend the poor and the sick.

Sonia Don't look so miserable. You're bored? Okay. But boredom is infectious you know? You've infected Ivan already, look. I've got so lazy. And I really can't afford to get lazy.

Ivan What time did Alexander say he wanted us here, Sonia?

Sonia One o'clock.

Ivan One o' clock. Do you think he needs to tell us something terribly, terribly, terribly important? Is there something remarkable he needs to, what, impart to the world, Helena?

Helena It'll be something about his work.

Ivan   What work? He doesn't work. He writes bollocks all day and moans about nonsense and winds himself up into a jealous froth. That's not work.

Helena   Oh shut up, Ivan.

Don't you ever get tired of the sound of your own voice?

Ivan   I'm sorry, Helena. I know. I'm being a prick. Forgive me. I'm sorry. Please.

Friends?

I got you some flowers! I did! This morning! Bright yellow roses! Will I get them for you? They can be a token of our newfound friendship.

He leaves.

Sonia   Helena, there's something I wanted to talk to you about.

Helena   What is it?

Sonia   I love Michael so much.

I have loved him for six years now. I love him more than I loved my own mother. I hear his voice all the time. He comes here every day now. He doesn't even notice me. I try and find excuses to talk to him all the time. I look into his eyes. It's like I gaze into them. I can't stop doing it. I've got no pride left. Even the dogs know I love him. I keep telling them.

Helena   Okay. Does Michael know?

Sonia   He never even looks at me.

Helena   He's such a strange man.

There is one thing we could do.

I could talk to him.

Sonia   Oh.

Helena   I'd do it very delicately.

Sonia   Oh. Uh.

Helena   Will you let me, Sonia?

Sonia   Okay.

Helena   We'll just find out if he likes you or not. And if it's a no, he should stop coming here shouldn't he?

Sonia   Yeah.

She nods her head.

Helena   It's easier when you don't see them.

We should ask him straight away. He wanted to show me a map. Or chart. Or something. About the trees. Go and find him. Tell him I want to see him.

Sonia   Do you promise you'll tell me the truth?

Helena   Of course I will. The truth is always better than uncertainty. Even if it's a difficult truth. Uncertainty is just, it's terrifying.

Sonia   Yes. Yes. You're right. I'll say you want to look at his maps.

She goes to leave then stops as she gets to the door.

No. Uncertainty's better. At least there's hope.

Helena   What did you say?

Sonia   Nothing.

She leaves.

Helena   He's not in love with her. That's obvious. But just because he's not in love with her doesn't mean he shouldn't be with her. She's fairly bland looking. Yes. He's not exactly – A man of his age? She'd make an excellent wife. She's clever. She's kind. I see what she means, though. He is handsome. He's interesting. He's attractive. Maybe I should. I could never forgive myself. He comes here every day now. I know why he comes. It's because of me.

Michael   Helena.

Helena   Michael.

Michael   You wanted to see my maps.

Helena   You told me you'd show me them. Are you free now?

Michael   Yes. Yes. Of course, I am. Yes.

Did you go to university?

Helena   I studied at the Royal Academy.

Michael   I don't think you're going to find this very interesting, you know?

Helena   Why not?

Michael   Now. Look at this. This is a map of this district as it was fifty years ago. The dark and light green is the forest. Half of this whole area. This is the flora and the fauna. There are swans, geese and ducks on this lake. There used to be a phrase. There was a 'power' of birds. Birds of every kind. More than the eye could take in. There were sand plovers. And Vega gulls. Bitterns. And there were blue-winged warblers. Now. Here. Look. This is how it was twenty-five years ago. Even by then only a third of the place is in forest. The green and the blue colours are already paler. And so on. And so on. The birds started to disappear. The blue-winged warblers disappeared completely. Now. Let's look at this. This is the map of the present day. There is some green here. And some here. But its patches. It's a picture of decay. Within fifteen years. Less. It will be gone. And you will say. People say. The world changes. Culture changes. Old ways of life give way to new. It's what happens. I understand that. I do. And these forests will be replaced by roads. There'll be industry. Factories. Schools and people will be healthier and better off and better educated but that's just not true. That's not happening. It's not. Everything's been destroyed. Nothing has been created.

I can tell by your face that this is just boring to you.

Helena   It's not.

I'll tell you the truth. My mind's somewhere else altogether.
I'm sorry.

You'll have to forgive me. I need to put you through a minor
interrogation and it's making me embarrassed so I don't
quite know how to begin.

Michael   An interrogation?

Helena   Yes. An interrogation. But a fairly harmless one.
Can we sit down? It's about a certain young person. Okay?

Michael   Okay.

Helena   It's Sonia.

Do you like Sonia?

Michael   Yes. Very much. I have great respect and affection
for her.

Helena   Yes. But do you like her as a woman?

Michael *coughs, thinks.*

Michael   Erm. No.

Helena   Just two or three words more and then that's it,
we're done. You haven't noticed anything has changed about
her recently?

Michael   No. Not a thing.

Helena   She's in pain. She's suffering. You need to
understand that. You need to stop coming here.

Michael   This is –

I'm too old for this.

And anyway, I couldn't –

I wouldn't even have the time!

Helena   Okay, good.

That's a relief.

I've gone all red.

Michael   If she's suffering then –

I don't want her to suffer.

There's just one thing I don't understand. Why did you need to interrogate me like this?

Helena   What do you mean?

Michael   Please, Helena, stop giving me that look. You know perfectly well I've been coming here every day. And you know perfectly well why. You know who I'm coming for.

Helena   I'm really confused.

Michael   Well. What more can I say? You have me. You knew that without this pretence of an interrogation.

I surrender to you. Here. Take me. Have me.

Helena   Have you lost your mind?

Michael   Come on. You're playing it a tad too shy now.

Helena   Okay. I think there's been a terrible misunderstanding

Michael   I'll leave. I won't come back. Never again. But.

We can have one time.

Helena   Stop it. That's enough. Leave me alone. Have you lost your mind?

He kisses her.

Don't. Please, God, leave me alone.

No don't leave.

Michael   Come to the reserve. Tomorrow. At two o'clock.

She sees **Ivan**.

Michael   Ivan. Yes. Hello. Smashing flowers. Great
weather. For flowers. This time of year. With the, the, the
rain. And then sun coming out sometimes.

I'll just be –

He leaves.

Ivan   I saw everything, Helena.

Helena   You need to help me, Ivan. You need to persuade
my husband that we need to leave here straight away. Today.
Do you hear me?

I need to get away from here today, Ivan.

Alexander   Where's my wife? Where is everybody?

Helena   Oh my God.

Alexander   I hate this house. It's an enormous maze.
People head off. In all directions. You can't find anybody.
Helena!

Helena   I'm here, Alexander.

Sonia   Helena, what did Michael say?

Helena   Sonia. I'll tell you later.

Sonia   Helena. You're shaking.

Oh.

I understand.

He won't be coming here again, will he?

He won't, will he?

Helena   No. Not anymore.

Sonia   Okay.

Alexander   Sit down. Will everybody please sit down.

Sit down. All of you. Please. Sonia. Sit down. For God's sake.
You too, Maureen. Liam. Ivan. Come on! Very good.

Friends, Romans, countrymen! Lend me your ears.

As they say.

Ivan   You don't really need me here do you, Alexander?

Alexander   Ivan, I do. I need all of you. You especially.

Ivan   Why especially me?

Alexander   Ivan, What's the matter with you? You seem very irritable. Even more so than usual. If I've done anything to annoy you then all I can do is beg your complete and immediate forgiveness.

Ivan   Oh fuck off, Alexander. Let's just crack on. What do you want?

Elizabeth *enters.*

Alexander   My friends.

I'll make a start.

Ah! Elizabeth! I forgot all about you. Sit down.

An Englishman, an Irishman and a Scotsman walk into a bar.

Ha! Sorry. No. In all seriousness. This is actually rather a serious matter. I have gathered you all here, my friends, to ask for your help and for your advice.

I am an artist. A man of film. Of image. Of idea. Of feeling. I have always been something of a stranger to the practical side of life.

I'm old and sick and so it makes sense to me that I make some attempt to, what, put my affairs in some kind of order. The truth is that there is only one certainty in all of our lives. My life is coming to an end. I'm not thinking of myself anymore. But I have a young wife. And I have an unmarried daughter.

I cannot live in the countryside anymore. It's impossible for me. We weren't built for the country. But to live in the city on the income from this estate is impossible. So we need to find a way which will establish a constant, guaranteed, more or less fixed figure income. And I think, I think, I have found one. And I wanted to take this opportunity to submit my proposal for your attention. If we set the nitty-gritty details aside for one second, I'll just set out the general outline. As it were. Our estate has an annual interest revenue of under two per cent. My proposal is that we sell it. If we convert the money that we receive from the estate into stocks and shares, if we invest it, then our annual revenue will increase to somewhere up to six even seven per cent. And I think we may even have an excess profit which we could use to invest in a modest place on, for example, the Isle of Man.

Ivan   Sorry. Just a moment. I think I'm going deaf. Could you say that again please, Alexander?

Alexander   Yes. We can use the profit from the sale to buy an offshore house in the Isle of Man.

Ivan   Not the stuff about the Isle of Man. You said something else.

Alexander   I'm going to sell the estate, Ivan.

Ivan   Yes! That was it! I thought that was what you said! That's a relief. I'm not going deaf after all! You'll sell the estate! Brilliant. Brilliant idea. Just brilliant.

Er. Can I ask you? If you did that. What would me and Sonia and my mum do?

Alexander   Yes. We will discuss that matter when the time is right. But for now –

Ivan   Wait. Just a second. Something has become rather clear to me. Just now. Just this moment. Up until this very moment, it is suddenly clear, I have been thinking like an absolute idiot. Up until now I was labouring under the delusion, the delusion, that this estate belongs to Sonia. My father bought the estate as a dowry for Anna. And until just this minute I was naive enough to think that the estate would pass from Anna to her daughter Sonia.

Alexander   Yes. Of course, the estate belongs to Sonia. Nobody's disputing that. I won't do anything without her consent. I would go so far to say that this whole venture is entirely for Sonia's benefit.

Ivan   This is nonsense. This is all nonsense. Either I've lost my mind or, or–

No. No. No. Give me some water.

Nobody does so he fetches himself a glass of water.

Carry on. Finish what you were going to say. Come on then!

Alexander   I don't quite understand why you are getting so agitated. I'm not saying that my plan is perfect. If everybody is opposed to it then of course I'm not going to insist.

Liam   I have always, er, Alexander, not only revered the arts but in some way felt as though the arts were part of my family. My brother Gregory's wife's brother, maybe you know him, Darragh Coleman. He actually had a masters in the history –

Sorry.

Ivan   My father bought the estate at three-quarters of its value. He was only able to do that because I renounced my share in it for Anna. Because I loved her. I loved her. And then I worked. I worked like an ox for ten years and I paid off all the debt that was accrued when my father bought the estate.

The only reason this place is debt free is because I worked so hard.

I have managed this place for twenty-five years. I worked. I've sent you rent on the lease. Like some kind of steward. Throughout all that time you never once thanked me. No matter how tight our margins were I never failed to send you the rent.

Alexander   Ivan, how was I meant to know anything about anything like rent and leases? I'm not a particularly practical man, Ivan. You know that. I've just said that. You could have taken some of the rent off. You could have given yourself whatever you wanted. I wouldn't have even noticed.

Ivan   Are you suggesting I should have stolen from you? Is that what I should have done? I should have stolen more. 'Oh, poor stupid Ivan! If only he'd stolen my money, he wouldn't be the decrepit fucking beggar he is today. What a total prick!'

Elizabeth   Ivan! No!

Ivan   For twenty-five years I have been stuck here inside this place. Like a fucking mole. With my deranged mother. All we ever thought about was you. All day, every day, all we talked about was you and your work. We were proud of you. And at night, every night, we watched your films. We wasted out lives watching all your films. My God how I hate your fucking films.

To us, honestly, you were God. Like a creature from a higher order. We knew your films by heart. We knew every scene. Every line. I still know every line.

But now I see the truth. For once in my life. You call yourself an artist? You wouldn't understand art if it shat in your face. Your work is worth nothing. Nothing. Not a thing. You are a fraud. You have always been a fraud. You always will be a fraud.

No. No. No. No. No. I will not be quiet. No. Don't you fucking move.

I haven't finished. You have ruined my whole life. I haven't lived. I haven't. I've wasted my whole life. I wasted away. And it was because of you.

The things I could have done, and I never did. I'm talented. I'm intelligent. I'm brave. If I'd lived the life I could have lived I could have been a Bresson! I could have been an

Ozu! I don't know what I'm saying. I'm losing my mind. Mum. I'm lost. I don't know what to do. Mum, please.

Elizabeth   What you need to do, young man, is pay attention to Alexander.

Ivan   I know what I'm going to do.

(*To* **Alexander**.) You won't forget me.

He goes out.

Alexander   What was all that about?

He's deranged.

He needs to leave here, and he needs to leave here now.

He is a nothing. He's nothing.

Sonia   You need to try to be kind, Daddy. Just try to explain to him what you meant.

Alexander   Alright! Fine! I'll go and explain myself to him.

Ivan *enters with a gun.*

Alexander   Stop him! Somebody stop him! Help me! He's lost his mind!

Helena   Give me the gun, Ivan. Give me the gun. Give it to me.

Ivan   Let me go, Helena.

Where the fuck is he? Ah. There he is.

Bang!

Did I miss him? Did I miss him?

Oh, my fucking God, My God. My God. Fuck. Fuck. Fuck. No. No. Stupid. Stupid. Stupid. Stupid. I fucking missed.

Act Four

That afternoon.

The house.

Michael *and* **Maureen**.

Liam   You should hurry up, Maureen. They'll be giving us a shout any second to say goodbye.

Maureen   I'm nearly done. I'm nearly done.

Liam   They're going to Lille. They're going to live in Lille.

Maureen   It's for the best, Liam.

Liam   They got into a right old state. Helena said, 'I can't live here for a single second longer. We're leaving. We're leaving right now. We can go and live in Lille.' Those were her exact words. I have no idea why she is insistent on Lille.

Maureen   All for the best. Guns. Jesus. It's a disgrace is what it is.

Liam   It's ironic when you think about it. Because it was like something out of a film.

Maureen   Not a film I'd like to watch. Things will go back to normal. We'll have breakfast at eight. Lunch at one. Dinner in the evening. Like normal people do.

Liam   I was going through the village this morning. The man in the newsagents was outside his shop. He saw me. Shouted at me. 'Is that you on your way to your Sonia's again is it, Crater? Got yourself your own little personal food bank there haven't you?' It was extremely hurtful.

Ivan *and* **Michael** *enter.*

Ivan   Michael, leave me alone. You too, Liam, for fuck's sake. Maureen. Can't everybody please just leave me alone for a minute. I can't stand this. Being watched over.

Liam Of course, Ivan. Right this second. I'm on my way, Ivan.

Ivan Good. Thank you.

Maureen You, Ivan, are a silly little sausage. A silly little sausage.

She leaves.

Ivan Michael, I told you to go and I meant it.

Michael I'm not going until you give me back what you took from me.

Ivan I've not taken anything from you.

Michael Okay, I'll wait patiently for about two more minutes and then I'm going to use force.

Ivan Fine.

Michael Fine.

Ivan Good.

Michael Good.

Ivan I made such an idiot of myself.

I shot him. Twice. I missed him. Twice. I'm never going to forgive myself for that.

It's funny. When you think about it. I'm an attempted murderer. But nobody's doing anything. They've not called the police. They're not trying to have me arrested. That must mean that they think I'm mad. Ha! That *I'm* the mad one?

I saw you.

I saw what you did with her.

Michael Yeah. I know you did.

Ivan I'm so ashamed, Michael. If you had the slightest idea how ashamed I feel.

Can you imagine if it was possible to completely change the way you live your life? To look at your life and ask yourself what you would do if it died. If your old life died. It ended. And then take what's left of your real life and live it properly. How can I do that, Michael? Where do I start?

Michael   This is just a distraction. You're distracting me. Come on. Give it back, Ivan.

Ivan   I haven't got anything.

Michael   You took a bottle of morphine from my case. Look, Ivan, if you're determined to kill yourself then just go into the forest and shoot yourself in the face. But give me the morphine back. Or people will blame me. They'll say I gave it to you. I don't need those rumours.

Sonia *enters*

Michael   Sonia, your uncle has taken some morphine from my medicine case and won't give it back.

Sonia   Uncle Ivan? Did you take his morphine?

Why do you do this to us?

Give it back, Uncle.

Please give it back. You're such a good person. You have to stop doing this to me.

Ivan   Here. Take it.

I have to get back to work, Sonia. I have to. And soon. If I don't get back to work soon, I don't know what I'll do.

Helena *enters*.

Helena   Ivan. You're here.

Ivan   Oh God. Helena.

Helena   Please will you go and talk to Alexander? There's something he wants to say to you.

Sonia   I'll take you, Uncle. You and Dad have got to make friends in the end.

She and **Ivan** *leave.*

Helena   I'm leaving, Michael.

Michael   Already?

Helena   We're all packed.

Michael   Right. Right. Right then.

Helena   Goodbye then.

Michael   Yes. Goodbye, Helena.

Did you get scared, did you?

Helena   I just want to ask one thing from you. I want you to respect me more than you do. I want you to respect who I am and what I want and the decisions I've made.

Michael   Just stay. Please.

He goes to kiss her. She angles her head so he kisses her cheek.

Okay. That's okay.

Helena   I wish you so much luck.

Oh for once in my life.

She throws herself at him. They give themselves to one another then back away.

I have to go.

Michael   Yes. Go. Go now. Right away.

Helena   Someone's coming.

They listen.

Michael   And so it ends.

Alexander *enters with* **Ivan**, **Elizabeth**, **Liam** *and* **Sonia**.

Alexander   I could write a film about all this! A film about how one should live a life! I accept your apology completely, Ivan. I only hope you find it in your heart to forgive me too.

Ivan   We'll keep sending the rent, Alexander. Don't you worry about that!

Everything will carry on as it always did.

Alexander   Goodbye, Elizabeth.

Elizabeth   Alexander, do you remember those photographs I took of you and Anna at her piano. Will you send them to me.

Alexander   Yes, of course.

Elizabeth   Thank you.

Liam   Goodbye, Alexander the Great! Please. Don't forget us!

Alexander   Goodbye, Liam. Goodbye, Elizabeth. Goodbye, everybody. Thank you for your company. I respect you all so much. But. Please. Let me say one thing to you. Do those things you most urgently need to get done. People should always do the things they most urgently need to get done.

Helena   Goodbye, Ivan. Ivan? Ivan? It's me. Helena.

Ivan   Goodbye, Helena.

Helena   Are you not going to wave me goodbye, Ivan?

Ivan   I can't.

I need to –

He turns and leaves. **Elizabeth** *and* **Sonia** *follow him.*

Alexander *leaves.*

Some time.

Maureen *comes in.*

Maureen   They've gone!

Sonia *comes in.*

Sonia   They've gone. I hope their journey's okay.

Uncle Ivan. Let's, er. Let's get some of this done, should we? Yes. Back to work.

It's been so long since we sat like this.

These pens have all run out.

I've got all sad. Now they've gone. It's funny.

Sonia   You do these. I'll do these.

You okay, Michael?

Michael   I don't want to go.

Sonia   When will we see you again, Michael?

Michael   I don't know, Sonia. In the new year, maybe. But – If anything happens. Medically. You will let me know. I'll come straight away.

Thank you for looking after me. And being so lovely to me.

Maureen   You've not had your tea, Michael.

Michael   I'm fine.

Maureen   How about a 'drink' drink?

Michael   I could do a quick one.

He drinks.

Well. I wish you all so much love. And luck. And all things. Don't see me out, Sonia.

He leaves. **Sonia** *follows.*

Sonia *comes back.*

Sonia   He's gone.

Maureen   Jesus.

Sonia   What can we do, Uncle?

We've got to live.

We'll keep living, Uncle Ivan.

We'll live through all these endless days. And these endless, endless nights. We'll take whatever life throws at us. We'll work. We'll do what needs to be done for other people and we'll do that now and we'll keep doing it until we get old. And when it's our time we'll die. And then. Only then. In those last minutes. We'll see our lives and we'll see what they were for. We'll see that our lives hurt and that we cried our hearts out and it was so hard, but it was in our nature. Uncle Ivan, my beautiful uncle, everything has its nature, and our nature is to try and to never stop trying and then, in those last minutes, we will see that our lives are beautiful and dignified and it will fill our hearts. And we'll look back at how unhappy we are now and we'll smile and we will laugh. I really believe that, Uncle. I believe it with all my heart.

We'll understand.

We'll see the whole sky full of diamonds. We'll see all the horrors of this life and this world, and all our pain dissolving in the grace of the Universe. And we will understand that our lives were quiet, gentle, sweet as a touch. I believe that. I believe that so much.

You're crying. Real tears. You haven't had a happy life, have you? But just wait, just hold on a little while longer. Just wait.

We'll understand.

We'll understand.

Printed in the USA
CPSIA information can be obtained
at www.ICGtesting.com
LVHW010228110324
774109LV00009B/655